Born in Sardinia, Italy, Samuele Zara has been living in the UK for many years, which he considers his beloved home. He is a professional actor, an eclectic practitioner of many different arts, a lover of the English Language and Literature, and a student of humanistic disciplines.

This collection of poems, conceived as a secular and spiritual journey, is his debut in the literary world.

He lives in Scotland.

You can find more about him and his works on his official website:

www.samuelezara.com

To all Men and Women
in search of meaning,
and to the Spirit.

Samuele Zara

# INDIGO ASHES

AUSTIN MACAULEY PUBLISHERS™

LONDON • CAMBRIDGE • NEW YORK • SHARJAH

A CIP catalogue record for this title is available from the British Library.

ISBN 9781398449305 (Paperback)
ISBN 9781398449312 (ePub e-book)

www.austinmacauley.com

First Published 2022
Austin Macauley Publishers Ltd®
1 Canada Square
Canary Wharf
London
E14 5AA

# Cast Away

Amongst rock awash
And sharp pale stones
I've travelled  my way,
Beaten by the waves
Thrown by the wind.

I've ruined and revolted
Tore my hull apart
Inside my guts,
Breaking my heart
Breaking it into the stones.

And I've slowly waited
The rotting of the corpse
After the storm
Under the sun.

Empty eyes turned up high
With no voice for a prayer
With nothing
but the memory to have had.

Then a music came softly from the East
It was like liquid light
or maybe it was just the Sun,
The head was still
All was still.

And a tear came
From the soaked eyes,
I was crying
And I wasn't dead.
I wasn't dead anymore.

# Rising

A tear emerged,
New water and new spring
From the rocks' hardened gash around my heart,
Appeared as a gift
Unexpected as summer rain.

Maybe it was You
Maybe it was me.
But slowly was rising and from Time was falling
And nothing was scaring me anymore.

# Ropes

For too long now
these stretched ropes
have been loosened.

For too long now
These ropes lie
Tired and entangled
As the cable on the wharf
After the sunset.

Just the floor seems to stop the fall
Towards the grave,
By all recanted 'no'
And all 'yes' never told.

# In the Dust

You cast us away
here
between Sky and Earth
and asked us…
What did you ask us for?

Your Voice has been heard by few
And how could we trust them?
Are they not animals that eat and defecate too?
We are so much distant from each other
That we'll never reach perfection.

But it is enough
For You.
Spitting blood,
Eating dust and mud.
For this You have created us
And we can't live otherwise,
We think we deserve this.

Too many shadows have been seen
In this dark cave,
And the light outside
Is just another deceptive Universe.

# Requests

What do You want again?
What do You want from me?
Myself?
My blood in my veins?
My life?
My memories?

What do You want from me again?
Tell me
What do You want
Again?

You have taken everything from me
My time
The body that I am
My years
The hope for a future.
Do You want my identity?
Do You want to hold me in your fist?
Do You want war?
It is just me
Me against You
The very Yourself.

And I'll cry and I'll smile
If you want this so
You make the rules.
But please
I'm asking You just one thing.

Give me the strength to challenge You
To defy You

To fight You
To believe to destroy You,
Because not always
I believe I will be able to do it.

# Rain in the Cracks

Slowly was pouring the rain
Lightly  was pouring
And the rocks washing.
Why not even a drop washes the cracks of my heart?
Why doesn't pierce in the deep
In the memory
And tear from their cracks apart
These rough oppressive claws,
These  acid mirrors of madness that break
That fall against the compulsion to fly away
From these chains of pity and regret?

Rain
Are you alive?
Could you hear me?
Crush me Sky
And send me high
And blow me as a dynamite
On the blue Infinity.

Destroy the guilt to be human
The memory of the gone days
The memory of the flesh
And leave me with just a few pebbles in one hand
And in the other
A little shard of faith.

To foolishly tremble myself
In front of All of This.

# Heaven on the Streets

How is it possible that You are so far away?
So far away that You seem to be just like a dream?
How many miles
Years
And maybe lives?
Your voice is the Light
Dawns and Sunsets of everyday of this time.

Who has divided us?
A fear dwells on the heart's gorges
Is it mine the guilt to have lost You?
Or it is just a thread
That indissolubly binds us
through the fogs of time?
The music and the chants
Are like the far-away sea
Neat remembrance before the first cry.

Who were we?
Who are we now?
Once again I want to see You
Before my time would be worn-out
And Death will set us up
For a new birth.

# Like Music

You are like music,
Like millions of orchestras contained in an ocean shell
Like millions of mermaids upon the ruins of old Atlantis
Like the songs of whales singing in the silent abysses,
Like the beating of my heart
Like the journey of my feet and the stillness of my voice,
Like the fist of my hand
And a sight lost into the Infinity.

Like the strength
which without I would be asleep
my waking up would be useless
and my sleep
eternal.

# As a Sparrow

So sweet was the memory of You
When tormented by rash becoming
I took shelter in You.
With trembling I was sheltering in You
As a sparrow between twisted Oak's walls
Away from a hasty cold Winter's storm.

But You Yourself were Snow
And Tempest
And Storm
And the Oak in which I took shelter
And I didn't know of it.
And I was sleeping
Between Your vast colossal feet.

# Arcane Cogs

From hungry doom's worn-out ashes
Reborn new life.

The ancient desire
Of the glare and the shade
Of the Light and the Dark,
Of opalescent shapes
Inlaid in landscapes,
Of vision and mysteries
On the brim of stories out of the Time
And erudite notions of arcane knowledge.

The well-oiled cogs have started again
Their round movements.

# Shades

What is this thing
That I'm about to reveal?
Billions of shades threatening shining
Between polished screens of unheard thoughts.

Is everything what that is
Just what that is?
In the cruel formulation
Of a comfortable mental reality
Still I find space to look for you.

But You have always been here.

New strength I have found in a bunch of rusted keys
Between the furious talents of unexpressed skills
With no more space and time.

My voice is just a shard of memory
The pale snapshot light
Of the already dead life's negative.

Everything is just a memory.

# Call

What dark feeling is looming in the air
And calling on my name?
What's echoing on this skin
On these bones
And still not be heard?

The silent music of the cells
Between the infinite spaces of emptiness
Reclaim the right exultation of my own existence.
Something is living unbeknownst to me
On the unconscious control of my every part
I don't know the fate of the flesh that I am.

And I am so heavy
So pushy and irking,
On the space that I'm filling
The time has lost faith
And the memory of the past seconds
It's worth already for an unknown existence,
Suddenly it seems I weigh like all the Earth
And just a feather holds myself.

I don't know why I'm still flesh
Just a thread stops me from falling.

# Hymn of a Dream

So it appeared
So old but so new
The impetuous stream of my desire.

Unexpected rising
On my backbone
On the legs
On the arms and head
a joy of life's intense chill.
For too long lost
In the whirlwind I've been swept away,
I just believed I was lost forever
Just forever.

But new joy reborn
Upon these friendly waves of distant notes,
Fellows of my journey
The music of my desire
The living notes of my becoming.
I renew my oath through her voice,
I push forward my brightness
Through the fogs of Space and Time
It is me who is flowing through these notes
It is me.

No hesitation on this gift's surrender
No bequest on the dream that I possess.
I've crossed the Death and Silence's mountains
I've caught sight of its touch
The unbearable loneliness
As someone who has never existed.

I've felt on my skin the heaviness
Of the body that I was and am
I've swum without pause oceans of fears,
And crawling
Standing still I am.

But I won't yield moving backwards
From Life's calling.

Never again scared
I will run away
In secret
Taking refuge
In the caves' gorges
Of a cowardly worthless ego's convoluted darkness.
Not anymore confined
On the soaked rotten chains
Of thought's without an owner.

This is my chant
The Life's hymn that flows
And go back no more
The hymn of a dream that I won't stop dreaming.

# A Ring Swears Somewhere

A ring swears somewhere
In a house.

Roaring
Rumbling scooters run.

How many are they
In this dirty city so grey?
Where are they going with no end?

Banging forks on ceramic plates
And too much speaking.

Voraciously eating.

# End of the Day

I'm just waiting for the end
The end of this day.

On the uninterrupted
Shaken rotten walls
Of bubonic sickening things
I repel
This empty reality's disconnected present.

Are old these places
As a rusty thing of scratching thinking.

# Funambulist

This is the wail
I know its smell,
Sadness is for poets rain
She dies wet on the heart's flames of pain.
But after that
Joy comes
As the sun
After the rain.

It doesn't seem too long
When I used to speak to you
And we were clashing against each other
The ludicrous armies of our hearts and minds.

On the tangled events I'm leaping
As funambulist with no net
Upon the dangerous game of emotions.

It's hard being a sponge
Poor empath
But don't care
It's always the same.

# Three Minutes

Everything flew too fast
Too much.

This morning three minutes seemed hours
And now
They are just memories
On the turning of an instant
That just before
Seemed eternal.

# Thud of Leaves

Everything is so wearing vast
Here and everywhere I turn my look around
For endless miles I can't see anything but
The unintelligible certainty
Of the fathomless All.

We are just that instant
Between the breaking of a stem
And the falling
Of the muffled thud of billions of leaves
Died unheard at night.

# Reborn

Reborn my child
Too long you have slept
Under ashes of regret.

Reborn!

Now is time to be big
Time to be and to have.
I've buried for you
The illusions of the ages,
In the darkness
Buried the endless sadness of hours
And under an Oak I've found
The crackling shining of the present time
The shining of the Water-Thought.

Reborn!

This is the time of the beginning
Time for freedom and life
And no one will hurt you again.

Because now I know
And now you know too.

# Wind's Void

Gently I cling to myself
On a wind's light void.

Slowly everything seems to collapse,
Every part of me
Has no connection anymore.

Just a thought make myself unite
But for not too long I will stay connected.

# Flares

I apply the law
Of unborn remnants
On the treading interpositions
Of evening's grievous flares.

Deadly I cling
To the dragging space
Of dormant apparitions.

# Space's Ghosts

I chase the unwilling space's ghosts
And buckled myself up
On the emotions' deceitfulness,
Ready.

On the impact to the uncertain
I take position
As a disloyal moralist.

# Senseless Days

In the unforeseen advance
Of actions and reactions
Sick habits stand.

In the wicked reflux
Of fluxing and refluxing
on swollen belly's dirty waters
there's just another obese flabby existence.

Hungry elapsing each other
Closed pressing one upon another
Demented banal declarations
Of days' senseless useless creations.

# Changing

Suspended.

Biting lucubration in middle air
I reduce every logic
To the ambivalent cheering
Of an uncertain scorn.

Dismayed by the living thought
I'm in the centre
Between what I seem
And what it seems around me.

I don't have any more
For a long time any more
Any mould of my human form.

The mirrors between mirrors
Are breaking
In the dirty house of older mirrors.

I reflect on every second of the shape-shifting thought.

I'm nothing
But the changing.

# On Grey Streets

I drag my desire
Floundering between the illusions' sharp brambles
Of strange and unpleasant disappointments.

Here
Too many grey streets around
Too many to bear
And it's unaware
The solution to this problem.
Too many screams sprinkle these places
As flowers' petals dispelled on the evening sun,
Too much noise relentless resounds
As someone who is merciless.

Nobody opens his own eyes dazzled by the darkness
Nobody understands the moment's importance
On the entangled skein of the silence's destiny.

As the Earth I'm waiting for the Rain,
The upcoming
Of the Final Truth.

# A Butterfly in Green

Is not giving up
The calling of the Earth,
She has not given up.

Unhealthy pressing the unreasonable occurring
Of the dark understanding's human greedy devouring.
The virus human doesn't appease his running
Degenerates to the bubonic tumour which is himself.

All is feeble
As the coloured rim of a butterfly in green,
The present instant is the reflection
Of which far away is dying.

I'm unaware if I'm going to survive
Or innominate dying amongst the nameless masses.
Slowly I wait for the coming of the rays
Between white walls of a hotel room.

All is ready in the New and in the Ancient,
Is coming.

# Blue Voice

In the Water's throbbing blue voice
I behold the Light outside
And a chant between reflections claims
The unheard advance of the Creation.

# Silent Thoughts

Given as  waterfalls of rivers on fire
Silent thoughts dive,
In the time's spaces there's no offence.

And they are pregnant
Of illusions of innocence.

# Fog

Trembling shivering soldiers
Boundless expanses of armies
Liquid armours
Reverberating and shaking
In the evening chalybeate lights.

# Farewell

On the door's light cleft
Your farewell tired eyes
Have returned the wave of my hand.
And you kissed me close to my mouth
Looking somewhere else
Thinking of something else.
Clouded sky loomed
And I admitted
I've avoided
And denied.

Your white caresses of scattered fates
I've reached and lost,
Past lessons set
On the shadows of virgin days.

Vain temperance with rays you wrapped around me
Lewdly sings my insubstantiality
Which crosses over and shines through
These crazy gestures of mine
Perpetual falling
With happened tears.
Deadly I sink
These deciduous limbs
On the density
Of crackling appearances
And the sound is ready
To sing the silence.

# Taken Away

I've been taken away from every understanding
climbing stairs of heaviness
Blind about the direction to follow.

I've been dying
To every distant phone call,
Unable to breathe
The bones were grievous
And muscles as tied as grease
Pressing every purpose
As the coal on the miner's back.

I was just the pale copy
Of what I was supposed to be,
Loneliness
Was just another face
Of my conceit,
And eating
Just a mocking substitute
Of that thing called Love.

# Mother

A life's cry
On my mother's face,
On my chest.

Discoloured lacquer
On the farewell knob.

# Basting

Basting
Feeble iniquitous wefts
Cramped imprisoned in other's glances
To confine
One's own consubstantial existence
To the roughened conventions
Of worldliness.

# Moon Witch

City's ghosts
Are dressed in turquoise and chalcedony
Upon the dancing blankets
Of nocturnal ponds,
And my hand on your face
Is near and far away.

On the glance of centuries
Tangos are armies
That move
the realms of our passion.

Teach me to find the light,
Living witness
Of my present humanity.
With no logic I abandon myself
On this blinding shroud
Of this waxing moon's celestial gorge.

My sweet deadly witch with wavy  hair
Your gown is nakedness
That is covered with mystery.

# Storm's Waves

I'll believe
In the bursting whisper
Of your sweet symphony.
I will sail on your words
Sweetly cuddling myself
As a happy shipwrecked man
In the ocean of his own wholeness.

Are your words
Or mine
What I'm longing for?

Close and far away
Your arrows tear my heart apart
And this your words' music
These storm's waves
Are mighty percussion.

# Peebles from the Void

It is something rare
As snow in August sands.

On distant shores
Clinks like armours
Under shiny stars.

And I dream of deserts
And paths of roses and thorns
Disentangling as snakes.

Amongst white ivory rocks
Soothingly moans
On silent winds.

# Drawing

In every silence's equation
Of every splinter of quiet
Between a bell's toll and a break for dinner,
The resolution
Is the Love for Everything.
Every person
Image
Thing
Is an arcane device of secret profuseness.

I stick up to the walls
rustling remembrances,
I make heaps of them
Through which I make bridges to Eternity.

Doubts are cowardice's faces,
Resume the journey
Resume the journey.

Sculpting carving the Light
On Trees that have been alive,
Impressing the corporeal concreteness
On ephemeral visions
Of crimson pigment.

I dress myself with Infinity
I switch on with memory
I glitter
I blaze up.

# Four O'clock

Barely four o'clock
Still I am the slave of my dreams,
Still a cloud in my heart
And lighting and tempest
And rains that cry from the past
As trickles of a waterfall
Upon lily's expanses.

I've got an engine in the skull
And white-hot memories' bolts
And smells of peaches
And songs of death
And dust
And echoes of dew and blood
And cold and hot words as a woman's lips
And her opiate smiles
As chants of nymphs and mermaids.

Leave me alone
Let me be foggy.
I'm not from all of you,
I'm not from the others.
I'm from theirs and from myself
I'm from the Silence and the Scream.

# Toaster

Rotten rickety corpses confined
In deep murky pits of other times.
Legacies of ancestral challenges
Slaughters,
Hideous massacres committed
to the most defenceless living beings.

Innocent and harmless
Certifying now the enormous blame
That once to him was done upon
And now immovable lain
On the memory of what had been.

In the dark bottom
Of a rusty toaster.

# Women's Voices

Lovely young women's voices
On the outstretched reefs of my soul
As billows they break the night.

Listening to
I greet these waves with clear innocence,
Words from a song
The only companion from a distant sunken past.

These are heart's hiccup's knots
Composed words on my emotions' score
On the unexpected music
Of all my happenings.

I was chains in a time not mine
In a body not mine.

# TVs

The TVs on
Are lucid bitterness,
A certain changed despair
of beats and percussion.

With too much feeling this soul is afflicted
Every voice is an emotion
Every music a shake
They besiege my passions' veins.

My old age shines through my child's eyes,
I'm still waiting for the time
When everything will be done.

# Redemption

Was pouring upon the naked muscles
Of the body that I am,
Was falling as redemption
Cold fallen drops
From a summer night sky.

The Wind in the air
Was shaking
Invisible coming.

# On a Steel Box

I let myself be carried
On this unavoidable ride
Of this steel box
Disguised as a vessel.

Smell of grass cut in the morning
Sun up high in the sky
The metal music
Eating my ears.

# Grey Lakes

Led by the interrupted scores
I've been shown the life
On the mocking Fate's palm.

I behold the Sky
Changing,
And the changing dream
That drags my name.

Peace is the lakes dyed of grey
Between the waves.

# Dark Princess

The archetypical wefts
Of your nocturnal hair
Vehemently bear
Iridescent engravings
disclosing inscriptions
of arcane unknown words.

Your skin is an expanse
To walk in it
As soft Greece soil
As Indian shores
As the Sahara's hot sands.
It tells my heart
The novels of your lust,
As the peaches' peel
Under a shadowy arbour in summer
And walnuts and strawberry's pulp.

As on vibrating glares
Of mountain's creeks
Your words echo
And your balmy gaze blows
As the Mistral Wind
On a summer sunset,
As the South Wind
On an October Night.

And I in you live
My love
And in the world
As in a dream with no wake-up,
As the first time
The life.

# A Silence's Gift

A fly dances
On inert limbs.

Undone sheets
and undone pillows.

A Silence's gift
From the world given.

# Obsidian Tapirs (In the Bathroom)

Powerless I've beheld
The peremptory silent crossing
Of gigantic
Enormous obsidian tapirs,
With black paws
And long horns,
On the white slops
Of high and erected cliffs.

And it seemed I heard
Their rummaging
Amidst vermilion carpets' silken dunes,
As huge as elephants
Eastward.

I've cheered them
In vain.
With no answer I've seen them
Disappearing,
Under white marble towers.

# Splinters

Vast turquoise and quartz skies
Painted as snow
On the shiny glasses
Of gloomy city cars.

The body is the sum
Of the memories that have been,
The sounds and lights of an iridescent sea
Spread as a shroud
Upon the Soul's present moment.

The lost legacy of time
Is the ineffectual resolution
About these our nowadays uncertainties.

In the comfort of friendly lovers
Fear and pleasure are fugitives
From a body on a cold winter day.

My dances
On this sweet bitter sea
Are dispelled splinters of imagination.

# Skin

I am the skin
Dressing these wrecks' carcasses
A dissonant metal
Between roaring of engines
And heinous contraptions
Further conditions
Cancelled by the improbable.

I pour myself onto the streets
With the music eating my ears
Welcomed by a new fate in my heart
In the abandon that crosses the thoughts.

A woman's image
paints my dreams
And redeem my soul
Converting my essence
In a laic religion of life.

# Speak to Me

Speak to me again
Upon the note's vibration
Radiantly pouring
As from crystalline spring
From Infinity's mountains.

Tell me about you.

Disclose
Spite and doubts
And pour all on me
So that I'll be your ship,
And we'll sail together
Beyond turmoil's seas
Where the pain is no more
And together living again.

Pursue your noble winged soul's nature
So that the Earth would yield
Her sad anchors
And her heavy iniquity,
And you could celestially soar
On the sky's vaults
Amongst stars and clouds
And rare and precious flying over.

Speak to me again
Between abloom rose's voluptuary movements,
And your lips could tell
Sincerely
Cosmos' beauties,
And so
speaking about you.

# Forgetfulness

Spread sheets
On the life's lapel
Images engraved with blood
On the decadent folds
Of every discernment of mine.

As dead  I am.

I shake the memory's flag
On the crackling reflections
Of my being
Given to the oblivion's flames.

I forget who I am
And so
What I will ever be.

# Painted Love

Rain paints
Songs in the air,
Motionless nesting tables
Next to the window,
Brushes and spotted sheets
Silently singing
The power of our love.

We are two
We are one.

And I speak to you
About colours and sounds
When instead
I mean I love you.

# Winter Clouds

Grey loneliness
Shines through
Smooth shadows
Of a wintry cloudy sky.

Grant my plea
Of carnal monk,
I praise the sacred vespers
Of my worldliness.

# Blind God

A child plays a trumpet
That God doesn't see
And the rain blinds
The tender cloak
Of reality.

# Thunder

Speak to me Thunder
Your voice is a master,

Arcane guardian
Of ancestral memories,

Reveal to me the secrets
Of the laughing and the crying.

# Stopping

I stop.

I hear the rain
I see her fall.

All is halted
All is silent.

# Childhood's Mist

It seems so long
So far away,
Tides and sunsets
Risen in sunrises with no time
On the boundless expanses of the memories.

Moments overlapping
On the childhood's mists
Disclosing towards the body,
Laboured breaths
And placid drowsiness.

Until the moment
You discover yourself as an adult
With a hand full of debts
And in the other
Remorse and regrets.

Craving an opportunity
To redeem every mistake and sin
Killing
every maybe and but.

# Rest

Wrapped
In these warm blankets
Placidly I bask myself.

It's a cradle
Of soft and changing bars
Of marzipan.

# Song of the Dead Men and Dead Women

This is the song of the dead men and dead women
Who speak from their worldly score,
This is the song of the dead men and dead women
Who want to be children once more.

Not anymore long hours at the office to feed the prime
minister
Or in the queues to pay people of the same kind,
We want to live without an eye so sinister
That overlooks and controls our mind.

We want again to play and to dream
As we used to do in our childhood,
We want to be free to sing and to scream
And don't think about a shelter or food.

# Ransom

Little ants
Dragging an armless wreak
Of a rotten brushwood cockroach,
After the rain
On this grey August's day.

It seems to be
The very first day of my life
As I've never seen it before.
I don't know any of the reasons
Of my past sad suffering.

I'm a silent hunter
From the boundless expanses,
I'm permeating around
By the thin bonds
From what I'm seeing
And what I'm hearing.

Slowly I seize
Every pulsation
That could help me
To rise to life again.

Silent mist scattering out
Show me the way
Through the past's clouds
To elude everything in the end.

Destiny is just an amalgam
Convulsive and wicked,
A facetious game

Of weird and mocking rules.

I ransom my flesh and soul
With golden drops
Of worldliness.

# Prayers on the Rocks

They're bending
Under the wind's chant
They answer back with humble circumstances.

Thousands speak
Amongst mountains and hills' ribs
But they don't listen to.

The poet is an unconscious illusion
The useless word
Between Earth and Sky.

# Soldier Women

Women dressed
With green and leaves
And tied hair with a black hat,
Still so much youth
In their hands and eyes.

Waiting,
The war is waiting.

With black night eye-shadow
They grip bags with their left hands
And with their right
They grip death.

Who has always given birth and life
Is now the so sad parody
Of the killer called man,
Handing a gun
Against nameless foreign eyes.

# A Gnat

A feeble moan
Bashful start
With imperceptible tumult
On the shaken moors
Of the arm.

A monster
Just as little as a hair
Gives so much trouble
In the vast universe called body.

Faint and tiny entity
How much do you arouse the life of a man?

Invisible hassle
A thought
Is the same as a gnat.

# Arctic Visit

Unarmed corpses
With dancing appearances
Not a breath of wind moves them.

Ghosts of ice and rocks
Where has been hidden my own existence?

Black flora
Lap against dark shores
With words and memories
Uninvited.

A voice
Far away.

# Towards No Words

I'm seeing
Pale dark-blue landscapes
There
The long snake train outside
Snowy homes and silent words
With no way roads
And no telling ways.

Mist speaks everywhere
Like a warm soft coat
On the cold white-black mountains
Upon people
Blind until they sleep.

Ask
My heart.

No distant horizons outside
And in my head
A better chant
Sings for survival.

More and more grows
Blindly and proudly
Towards the right way of my end.

# Towards Boundaries of Stars

When time
Will deprive us
Of walks and summer nights
And the smell of burning stars
And the street lamps of distant towns.

When your hair
And your new always steps
Will be just the memory
Of a past youth,
Old age will carry us
Far-away
At the end of our era,
At the end of our story.

Maybe still together
Maybe different and apart
With regret of not having lived
Or simply
Not having lived enough.


Everything will fade and wither
On the upcoming uncertainty
Of a world that won't be this world anymore
on the wrenching fear in my heart
That you won't be anymore.

# November Trees

Are crying the trees
Of gold and majesty,
Of ancient they tell
Of auburn shining coat of arms
Green-bronze rare jewels.

Languid is their chant
As a caress,
Set gems
On the silver chromed crown
Of this early leaden morning.

Lucid November
As lucid as a blade,
Virginal armed waiting
Of a gloomy fight
And nothing.

# Onyx Night

Unarmed
Motionless a black dumb glove
Disheartened lies cries alone,
The lost mate
Among filthy opalescent spots
Of motor oil.

In the air
clamour of  surrogates
Of pastries' smell
Just released from the ovens,
Scornful placebo
Of a tomorrow morning.
In there
blindly they will drown themselves
Sad unconsciousness.

Luscious rolling shutter
Furtive impatient goes down
The forthcoming sex's smell
Happily seen through suffused lights.

The women's water
Taste of honey of a thousand flowers
And I deeply taste the taste
While I'm making love
Amongst memories' ravines.

# Kiss of the Sun

Presses and gropes
The solar wadding's touch
Golden blanket
On the sour roofs' crust.

The air is soaked
Of labour
scratches
and noises.

I've got some silence
Lying upon dear scattered sheets.

Mist and words
The hills seem still sleeping.

# Mud Heart

Today
I have no place in me.

In the heart
A sad meatus
Which tears apart
And plagues.

Motionless
Everything shines through
And my heavy weight of stone
Is the shadow of Death.

# Rippling

Ripple
On the shoreline of the morning
Sound's splinters
On the rebellious billows
Of luscious satisfactions.

Broken reverberates
The purity of your grudge.

# Afternoon

Blind
Are my ears today
And a deceit's dark mantle
Is wrapped around me
And on the lies of myself.

Inert as a black crystal
The world with no words lies
On the unarmed wadding
Of abducted lights
Of a fallen afternoon.

Their voices
Silently echoing
And I don't know
The minutes' future
And youth's theories.

I'm a diaphanous engraving
On a tired film
Of sour memories.

# In a Bunch of Keys

I admire the wefts
Of this cerulean silence
As ancient gems
Set on the boundless universe
Of my room.

Hidden vibrate wisdoms
In which with no doubt I could dive in
From the high cliffs
Of my powerless ignorance.

I paint in the air
Words with no sounds
On the oceanic walls
Of this intangible solidity.

Unexpected
On the interstellar distance
Between the stone of myself
And the door over there
At the end of the room.

I silently behold
The dumb gesture of God
Between my eyes
And a bunch of keys.

# Dances of Lies

I would quench my thirst
From the dryness of her silence,
Feed myself with the deaf songs of her voice
And plunge on the eternity of her smiles,
Light-years away
Light-years distant from me
As from the beginning of Time.

And my love is just a jest
A witty laugh
With a sour out of date battery's taste,
A joke of a wrong encounter
A dream of a destiny never happened.

Just a desert of trickeries and indifference
I have found on her waiting
In the besieged hours
Of this leaden rusty night.

Dumb is her heart
As the hitman of my verdict,
The sentence that I can't forget,
The cold warmth of her never come caresses.

Cursed be my memory
And the memories that don't shy away.

I melt this concrete dew
And sing to the void
Of a dead passion.

# Drops

Lost
On these faint identities of time
I lay my heart
Softly
Away from every world
From every forgotten road.

The comforts of the flesh
Are tranquil lullabies
Luscious skeins
Of death's greedy future sentences.

Memories resurface
Unexpected
As a fate's game
To show me shiningly the way,
Unblocking solutions
Of roads towards myself,
To take back interrupted melodies
When I was dreaming on a tiny bed
 Child's wintry dreams.

It seems that I was born today
This morning
Tonight.
New things to explore
New games to learn
No memories to remember
Everything to hope for.
I'm like one of these yellow leaves
Fallen as the others
Fallen together

with all the others.

I'm nothing special,
Just a leaf
yellowed by time,
Just a leaf
As the others.

# Song at the End of the Journey

Sometimes
I'm like the summer sea
On the evening,
When a deep red sun
Tired lies down
On a grand horizon
With memories thick.

On that deep-red instant
Bursts a fiery desire for revolt
And quickens
The urgency to live forever.
And distant echoes
the languid voice of the waves,
The whispers of the sand below my feet
And my prayers lost in the wind.

Crack a little then
The neon candlesticks
Of roads scattered more and more,
And are crawling the cars
As will-o-the-wisps of a leaden sepulchre.
They all are going to die
On their transparent beds,
Softening desperations
With fucking and TVs.

# Surrender

On secluded street's filthy shores
As virginal fairies with broken wings
With no voice and no chants
Gather homeless  and broken hearts
And youngsters without present
And men with no songs powerless lay
On the opalescent rivers
Of bottles already ended.

And so I still
Dejected
On the unexpected revelations
of things for too long suffered.
All the lost women and broken loves
My child's smile
My father's hug
My mother's voice
The plays and laughs with my brothers,
The choices never taken
The youth which will never come back
Everything that will never come back.

And yet
On this my heart swollen with absence
Brimful with emptiness and leavings
On these grey curtains of past resemblances
All that I can do is just surrender.

Mocked without grudge silently I lie
On the shore's blazing glare
Of this my sweet infinite soul.

# Just for You

If the Highest Force
Shouldn't compelled
Human bounds
On this feeble flesh,
And my bones and blood
Shouldn't be so fleeting
On this weak brim
Of this my little life,
I would move the mountains
With these very arms
To make you a secure bed
In which you could safely sleep
Sheltered from storms
And the inclemency of life.

Drop by drop
I would empty the oceans
And the rivers
And lakes
And the silent streams
And would make just one big vast sea
In which you could plunge yourself
And cleanse from all your fears and perturbations
And doubts of the heart.

I would run and dance through the stars
I would uproot their orbits
And the unchangeable trails
And a new starry sky
I would make on the heavens
So just your name would be written in the eternity
And everyone could admire and worship your beauty

And loving you,
And no seasons
No centuries
No aeons
No epochs and no civilisations
Could never forget you.

But I'm just a man
Only a man
Just a little mortal man
And just my love
I could give it to you.

And I regret life
And regret death
Because nothing
Will be enough
For everything you will always be.

# Night of Desires

I turn my eyes back
Just a little,
To the days' sunsets
That have beheld myself
So ancient.

Over the centuries' rivers
Glimpsed on the bend of the days
I'm extinguished
on the lapping
against out-of-reach longings.

Not even a week
And as aeons my voice is broken and silent
And a curtain of uncertain wadding
Has brought down the stage of my thoughts
And tiredly bent my limb's rush
On the weight of unbearable bitterness.

Barren fists and silent screams
I have thrown
Against mocking absurdities' walls,
Shattered is my will
Shattered is my memory.
How much I want
How much I wanted
And how much of you I still want.

I take the shards of what I was
Just a few days ago
Of what I was.

And I have just rubbles
And splinters
And stones
In front of my regret
Of myself that cannot
But, O Gods!
How much it would!

Man
Lover
Son,
Just shards
And diaphanous shapes,
Without your glance
Without mine
With no assurance of tomorrow.

Not even a whiff and an hour
That my heart opened to you.
Dear friend that I crave
you already are so far away and lost
Even before having you beside me.
And I crave the chances
Of myself that doesn't leave me
So everything is stopping
And a dam of dullness
Bars my advance.
On this night I'm still looking for myself
And I'm still looking for you
Which your faint memory on my dumb fists I try to grasp
And as sand
You slip away.

The  fearful wind of the days
will make me foreign to your heart
And powerless to my own.

I just bend my head

And silently I still.

With frock my sad soul is donned
And nothing could give
But its own chant.

# Ten Days

I follow
These  disdainful shreds of time
On the voracious throng
Interwoven with burdens
Of these broken heart's bones,
And trembling season
Of a future with no peace.

And I see our life
Beyond what could have been,
Different choices
Different roads,
Another you on some corner of a street
Another me.

If this inescapable past
Shouldn't have been taken from us
so hardly from our present,
so greedily voraciously murdering
depriving our days from our days
that were our right to live.

Who guess what future will have waited for us
Beyond that curtain of foolishness?
Ten days
Ten years
Ten centuries dispelled on the wind
Of all distant possible realities.

On the cigarettes' stumps
Begging breaths that taste of you
Foggy with all the kisses never given

With all the caresses never stroke
With all the sleepless nights,
I crave the lost illusions of you.
On memories tasting as unresolved prophecies
Predictions ripped off from the time's flesh,
Future's memories
That tear apart as angry wolves
My unarmed limbs
Of reasons without purpose
Of a soul with no rest.

I still find you
In those hidden realities
Where you still love me,
And everything is right
And nothing is wrong.

# Fallen Night

Fallen night
upon this blackened ice
By dint of leaving pieces of heart around
there is no longer of it
in me.

# Prophecies

I've seen prophecies
On couched fasten lands
displaced like swords
Throbbing waiting
For upcoming battles.

Among spring sentences
And breezes of whispers with no lies
I heard voices without voice
Smiting
Like a million of gloomy stones
In a shuddering remembrance
Of smoky curtains of omniscience.

# Floating

Floating
On the gloomy
Thick silence's giblets of the night.

Cars ghostly chattering
On the bathed rivers
Of space and time
Outside the window.

And in here
Peacefully I yield.

# My Night

All is quiet
All is peace.
I get back on my route
Placid I sail
On the Night's ocean's warm womb.

Outside
Not a breath of wind
Shakes the fronds
And I
Languid I surrender
To my eternal journey.

I am peace
I am desire
I am hope.
And I'm not afraid
Of the victory over myself.

Over there
Silently the Light and the Dawn
are waiting for me
And with eyes wet with joy I laugh
I laugh with no end.

# Shore of Love

I would like to have a shore
Kissed by the night's wisdom
And dive ourselves into her blazing shadow
Of the aeons of stars.

And making love you and I
Hand in hand
Till the dazzling dawn
Will discover us pure and naked
And will dress us with Infinity.

# A Tomorrow's Day

In the park
Embracing each other
Mine eyes in yours
Like on the first day of our first sight.
Sun throws warm hands
Upon our crowned souls,
Glad shadows draw
On the lush flowering grass.
Our children are laughing in the sun
And we are all spangled with tenderness.

They make smiles
And play games,
Happily running
Merely chattering,
Like young lions
They're breathing grace.
They are our daughter and our son
They are the queen and the king
Of wonderments.

We are still embraced
deep eyes
in each other's eyes.
We speak with smiles
We say no words,
All is alight
All is bright,
And queries and replies we don't need.

I would like it would be with no end today,
I would like to die

On a fair day like this.
But no
Not yet
not today.
With tears of joy
Is plenty my heart.

# A November Morning

I throw my heart
In the awakened morning
Through shimmering padding
Mottled by golden kisses.

I toss my soul
In the blinding yellow and blue
Stroked by black wings
Inked flock-friendly symphonies.

Sinking
My spirit I soak
With hopes,
warmed with the cold
of November,
scented with joy
painted with endless trust.

From a heaven full of silent laughs
I turn my sight on Earth,
and in the burning casket of my heart
I return,
And secrets I keep.

# Caducity

They devour themselves
at the end of the day
with kisses
voracious teenagers,
sheltered for a little
by the deadly illusions
of tomorrow.

At the corner of graveyards
rose sellers smile,
with tears
disguised in the eyes.

# Nocturnal Bedlam

On the Night's immaculate bosom
drenched in torments raise
the shaken boorish bedlam
of forlorn human meetings.

Wrapped in vulgar screams
creeps
on the sacred Silence's enclave
the venereal unconsciousness' disease.

Dressed with laughs
disguised are funereal exaltations
dripping ghosts
distilling unaware cowardly carelessly
proleptic putrefactions
of future sepulchral abodes.

Over here
the space's vault is blind
even these vapid houses' lights
dim those of the Stars.

# Placidness on the 5<sup>th</sup> Hour

On the night's vastness
Lost corners are revealed,
Soul's amputations
Torn mythologies
Waned memories
Belongings.

Fearful white-rabbits
Upon the vampiric hour
Sulphurous presence
Pistachio and almond flavoured
Inaction's bell towers
Dripping euphuistic euphemisms.

On silent tolls
I leap over the murderous indifference
Of past lovers
Stained with my past blood
Of my knelt naive heart.
Detached by now from their pawing ants
I smile at their sprung boxed clown's smiles.

Devoted to the moment
To the words and the silence
And to you.

Craved but unaware,
I throw bottles at the waves
And I
Placid delay
To this very sweet island
Of this dark hour.

# Worlds

Surviving
Dragging shouting
irrepressible worlds
Kicking lied
In chains
Under the weight of earthly foolishness
Of imposed customs.

Unspoken desires
Full of rage
Unheard
Yelling shaking
Under cryptic inconsistency
Of inconceivable masks of compliance.

# Entrails of Time

Night
Glaring bride
Accomplice
Of my oaths in disguise.

With eyes moulded in death
I stand,
Astonished grabbing
These rotten entrails of time.

I'm craving
For a future,
Dead so soon in the past.

Echoed
That child weeps
In a corner of the mirror,
And all is adrift.

# Treacle of Nails

Sour words
Hanged
To the gallows of pride.

Silences in ambush
weighed on
the barters of love
as treacle of nails.

Deadly plague
slowly sleeping
into our hopes of happiness.

We toast in the night
our murders disguised in whims
upon the corpses of our souls.

We are just spoiled children
playing with knives.

# Gates of the Past

Gates of old wounds
Are opening unrequested
Unexpected tonight,
And ample rivers of sorrows
Rabidly flow in the deep cracks of my heart.

Memories,
wrongly believed long lost forgotten
and buried in rituals of salvation,
Vivid resurface truer than ever
Truer today than yesterday
Like blood soaking from the soil of the earth.

Her voice clear now
Like the time she was still loving me
And I was the only one.
Her eyes joyful as never been
And on my chest and arms still I feel
Her warm embrace of her burning secure skin.
I've loved her inexplicably and beyond any reason
Beyond at the end
The dirty power of her lies and betrayal.
And yet it's still there
my love
Somewhere frozen in a distant faraway dimension,
Where she's still true and just
And we are still pure,
Like in a bubble
frail and transparent
in a storm of nails
Mucked by her lust and greed
Beyond repair.

Killed are now our innocent laughs
Annihilated our white kisses and hugs.
There won't be any more that happiness called us
Apart from these wrenching illusions of mine
Tonight,
Where my unstoppable tears don't cease
My ancient lost longing for you.

I call your name in vain
Conjuring a ghost from that grave of regret.

But all is dead
And my love for you is caged
In a prison of doves and mud
Guarded by hounds of unforgiveness
Don with immovable masks of hate.

You are just a shadow
Under my Sun's unwavering power to love.

# Road to Glasgow

White pale steel knights
Warding in the mist
Spanning to the sky
Slowly swinging fearful blades,
Confident warriors
In their ordeals of the morn.

Standing they are
As gigantic shrines of war
Of a distant alien world.

The trail ahead I follow
The dawn behind.
There is still hope today
And swarming thoughts
Don't blur my heart.

In the frosty haze
I throw my soul.

# The Blue-Green Teacups
## of Paradise

Out-of-tune songs fill the air
And clumsy teenage fingers
Play frozen guitars
On a winter morning that has still to come.

Merry-go-round endlessly
Twisting their turn of happiness
On giant blue-green teacups.

Smiles and laughs everywhere
And the red ginger hair of the women
Burns the chilly hair
Like a blessing of heaven.

I'm looking for her eyes
But they are inlaid in the future.
Now
Only mine are set on a shop window
And a faint smile
Is mirrored on the street.

# Howling Wind

Wind is howling outside the window,
Scattered seagulls
As outcast nymphs
Are crying their pleas for redemption
On a scourged rainy land.

Somewhere
Beyond the hill
Unheard the sea is screaming
His everlasting godlike fury,
My back is stiff from hard work.

A storm is coming
But silently I still,
Like a candle in the dark.

# Night Trees

Ravens are sleeping now
Ceased their ominous cawing
In the last shadow of the sun.

As mechanical ants
Slowly switching off
People are fading
In their coffins of TVs and concrete.

In the silence of the night
I hear the trees screaming.

# Distant Waves

Galaxies
And nebulas
And worlds
Trails and shines
Glares
And spirits in ascensions
Cleansed in oceans
Of intergalactic fires.

In a fortress without stones
Guarding flowers,
High on a mountain stands
A cross-legged child
With a light
In hands.

Parallel
Side by side
World by world
Claiming God with no shape
Endless faces and endless names with no name,
Inlaid in barks inlaid in stones,
Inlaid in leaves inlaid in skins,
Into the ice into the water,
Into the fire into the sky
Into the Soul
Without words.

The songs
Of the forests of the planets
Light-years and years away
And the chants of waves

Into which no man has never bathed.

Reflections in a lake
Of a mountain's peak
Purpled snow and green,
Two moons ripple
A gust of sulphur wind.

Ruffling of Gods
In clustered woods
And a saint in a shrine
With tentacles and claws
For a prayer joined.
With a jagged back
Bowed,
uttering invocations
Praying he lies,
a different prophet
for a different sin,
died.
Winged beaked humpback whales
Singing in nitrogen clouds
A blue sun in a never-ending dawn,
Lizards raising cathedrals on a creaked ground
Tangled cogs clicking around a star's crown.

Echoes
And crackling in the dark
And pouring of acid rains
Storms of dust,
A silence never ever heard.
Forces that move continents
With a blinking of a disembodied eye,
No claim to prove
No mountains for no man to move.

And flocks of jellyfishes
Immeasurable

Colourful dancing
On speckled lights of purple skies.

And then achest in a cave
With a scroll
Trillions of years old
Silently guarded
By a forgotten wrinkled speared guardian
Watching the sunset
Of a forsaken deserted planet.

# The Grass Is High on the Ground

The Grass is high on the Ground
With millions of green hands
She reaches the fair vault of the sky.

But the lawn-mower comes
With is greedy angry blades
Devouring those cheering lives
With dumbness and mechanical mind,
A bored guy possessed on steering-wheel
Smoking.

With noise and pride
Humans can't stand by Nature
They always want to cut,
Cleaning their gardens and city parks
They can't clean their souls and minds.

But the Grass is high on the Ground
And humans are mortal and deadly things.
When they all will be gone
Still the Grass will be high on the Ground.

# By the Wind

What voices are scattered
Hidden in the wind?

Inlaid
On this cold night
Stars pulsating somewhere
Hanged
On the bewildering schemes
Of galaxies adrift.

Other thoughts
Wandering out
From a different window
in the shadow of a different star,
Calling on a different God
For a different reason
Driven by the same Awe.

Billions and billions of windows
With looks thrown into skies blinded with stars
And voices
Carried by the wind.

# A Light Will Shine in the Dark

A light will shine in the dark
Revolting in the middle of the mass
A sound claiming the victory
The victory within.

Thousands of years
Crawling on the dirt
Confused by the words of the false
Just escaping
From faces in the mirror frame.

And wings will bring ourselves
Away in the skies
But with long
Unforgotten roots in the ground.

The pain will be our joy
And the glory of the sufferance
Will be the claiming of our understanding.
There will be Gods and Us.

And so we will finally see
We'll see ourselves
We'll see the people
And the true shape of a Tree.

And in the wind
We will understand its voice
And disclose its chant.

Because in the wind and in the clouds
We'll be opened

A light piercing in the dark
And our Soul will shine
Along with the rest of All.

# Stillness

There's no wind today
No voices on the day.
Trees stand still
No leaves move
No branches speak.

All the world is distant
Yet so close,
All the humans are far away
Yet still here.
All spirits dwell in their harbour of grace
And I
I'm shrouded in silence.

I wait
Alone
Yet not alone,
Encompassed by this present moment,
and there's no past in me
No future either.
I'm inside and outside
In this body
And in the clouds out there,
Waiting
Myself embodied
In a patient waiting.

A laugh sparkles in the silence
My heart pouring certainty
In the stark sea of doubts.

Now

Planted long ago
The seeds are slowly blossoming,
They are joyfully muttering
As a pack of playful cubs
Under the gloomy bed of dead leaves.

Life is crackling
Under the calm surface of the lake.

And I'm here
Yet I'm there.

And I'm alone
Yet not alone.